1 'Seeing the Pantomime.' From a hand coloured
stereoscopic slide, 1860

2 OVERLEAF Theatrical composite photograph by Samuel A. Walker, 1866

Victorian and Edwardian

ENTERTAINMENT

from old photographs

RAYMOND MANDER
AND
JOE MITCHENSON

B. T. Batsford Ltd · *London*

Other books by Raymond Mander and Joe Mitchenson

HAMLET THROUGH THE AGES

THEATRICAL COMPANION TO SHAW

THEATRICAL COMPANION TO MAUGHAM

THEATRICAL COMPANION TO COWARD

THE ARTIST AND THE THEATRE
The Story of the W. Somerset Maugham Theatrical Pictures

A PICTURE HISTORY OF BRITISH THEATRE

A PICTURE HISTORY OF OPERA
In collaboration with Philip Hope-Wallace

THE GAY TWENTIES
In collaboration with J. C. Trewin

THE TURBULENT THIRTIES
In collaboration with J. C. Trewin

THE THEATRES OF LONDON
Illustrated by Timothy Birdsall

A PICTURE HISTORY OF GILBERT & SULLIVAN

BRITISH MUSIC HALL: *A Story in Pictures*

THE LOST THEATRES OF LONDON

MUSICAL COMEDY: *A Story in Pictures*

REVUE: *A Story in Pictures*

PANTOMIME: *A Story in Pictures*

THE WAGNER COMPANION

First published 1978
© Raymond Mander and Joe Mitchenson 1978
Filmset by Keyspools Ltd, Golborne, Lancs.
Printed in Great Britain by
The Anchor Press Ltd, Tiptree, Essex
for the publishers B. T. Batsford Ltd
4 Fitzhardinge Street, London W1H 0AH

ISBN 0 7134 1257 7

Contents

3 Sandwich man, 1905

*Dedicated to the memory of those
behind the camera, known and
unknown, and their sitters who patiently
watched for the dickie-bird;
and personally to two Colins.*

Camille Clifford (Photograph: Hutchinson and Svendsen)

Acknowledgments

The idea had long been simmering in our minds to compile a collection of photographs on the subject of general Victorian and Edwardian Entertainments – especially those which had escaped the more specialised books on theatre and opera – and to demonstrate the rise and perfection of theatrical photography. Out of the blue, Sam Carr of Batsford suggested the very same idea as a volume for this series. We can only offer our thanks for this and for providing us with such a cooperative art editor as Peter Bate. We would also like to pay special thanks to David Hughes, who has become the Collection's Photographer Extraordinary, for having copied all the pictures from our own files in such an expert manner: old and faded originals needed great expertise and loving care to bring out the best that was in them.

Our thanks, as always, to Anthony Latham of the Theatre Museum (and one of our trustees) for all his telephonic assistance. Our thanks are also due to Colin Ford, Keeper of Films and Photography at the National Portrait Gallery, for casting his expert eye over our introduction; and lastly to Colin Mabberley, without whom the book would not have reached its final stages.

We have found the three volumes of *Living London* by George R. Sims (1902) particularly useful for some turn-of-the-century pictures. A special mention also to Ian MacLennan and Peter Thorogood for opportunely finding for us photograph number 167.

Unless otherwise stated, the photographs are from our own files, and are reproduced by permission of the Trustees of the Raymond Mander and Joe Mitchenson Theatre Collection. We duly acknowledge permission and offer thanks for the use of the following photographs: The Theatre Museum, Victoria and Albert Museum, Nos 16, 17, 24, 53, 54, 63, 67 and 142; The Victoria and Albert Museum, Nos 40 and 41; Bernard Price, Chichester, No. 110. Nos 108, 111, 152, 159, 162, 166 came from Batsford's collection.

Introduction

The Victorian theatre and its allied entertainments were quick to realise the value of photography as a medium for self-exploitation. While certain elder statesmen of the theatre who could have been caught by the camera in character, albeit in the studio, only preserved their likenesses in off-stage portraiture (for instance Macready who retired in 1851, of whom only elderly off-stage portraits exist), members of a younger generation like Phelps soon became immortalised by daguerreotypes, though only at second hand. Of the magnificent series of theatrical portraits taken of Phelps and his Sadler's Wells Company, which appeared in the various Tallis publications, no originals seem now to exist. They must have been disposed of as far as the publishers were concerned, once the engraved plate had been made. The steel engravings taken from these originals do however preserve the feeling of the original photograph. They were taken over a period of five years from 1845 (the daguerreotype was introduced in 1839) and the presumably one-and-only example of each was used by the engraver to produce the plates, which first appeared in *Tallis's Dramatic Magazine* (November 1850–June 1851) which was followed by the *Drawing-Room Table Book* and *Tallis's Shakespeare Gallery*. Most of the plates, with others of Phelps's contemporaries, ended up in various editions of Shakespeare's plays issued in parts up to the 1870s. The originals were mainly taken by Paine of Islington. We have not included any of these second-hand photographs, choosing to start our survey at a time when it became possible, in the early '50s, to reproduce

4 Itinerant photographer on Clapham Common, 1877
(Photograph : John Thomson)

any number of prints on paper from an original negative.

These new processes made commercial photography more practicable; studios opened all over the country, and it is at this period that our illustrations commence. We are letting the story of the multitudinous facets of Victorian and Edwardian entertainments, which appealed to all classes, reveal itself in the pictures and their captions, confining ourselves here to giving some idea of the role of the photographer.

Charles Kean was one of the first managers to take advantage of new processes. His *The Winter's Tale* and *A Midsummer Night's Dream*, both in 1856 at the Princess's, are the first record we have of theatrical costumes and groupings, though of course taken in a studio against miniature backcloths often closely copied from the actual stage settings. Many of these were also taken by the stereoscopic camera for use as slides for the Stereoscope, which was then becoming popular in the Victorian parlour. Some were hand coloured, an embryo of the short-lived 3D colour experiment in the cinema in post-war years. We have included one such slide in its entirety, but in other cases only one of the dual sides (left or right) has been shown. Often these slides of theatrical life (on and off-stage) were excellent montages or 'scenes' set up in the studio. Dual portraits, called Binographs, taken by double exposure, and triple ones also came into vogue.

The advent of popular illustrated journalism was of great use in exploiting entertainment. *The Illustrated London News* dates from 1842, and had several imitators, all equally dedicated to printing pictures of stage plays, opera and ballet, and they soon used photography as a basis for their wood engraving. The lithograph fronts of popular music often drew their inspiration from photographs from the 1850s up to the '90s. It was not until the invention of the half-tone block that the actual reproduction of the photograph in a magazine or journal could be achieved. Though mentioned in 1880 in America it was the end of the decade before reproductions of theatrical scenes began to appear in magazines like *The Theatre*; meantime, a commercial process called Woodburytype (permanent photograph) was used to mass-produce photographs in books, journals and theatre programmes. Woodburytypes were even sold as *carte de visite* portraits with an advertisement for Taunus Table

Waters on the reverse, vended from a penny-in-the-slot machine. The commercial sale of photographs of notables in all fields rose to large proportions as sizes grew from the *carte de visite* to the cabinet and panel portrait, only to be eclipsed by the introduction of the picture postcard at the turn of the century.

Among the earliest photographers to specialise in theatrical portraiture was Adolphe Beau. He has left some account of his work in a letter to Frederic Whyte which was included in his *Actors of the Century* in 1898. In it he says:

'Perhaps I might be allowed to mention my having been one of the pioneers of photography in this country? There were indeed very few photographers in London at the time when, with Silvy, I introduced the "full length *cartes de visite*". We thought the best plan for this purpose was to produce at first a series of theatrical portraits, thus enabling the public to judge what they would be like as regards likeness and artistic treatment. Therefore the studio of Porchester Terrace became the *rendezvous* of the most eminent of the "Profession". Later on, in my studio in Regent Street, I followed in the same strain, and I possess a most important and unique collection of the first dramatic portraits of the period.

'It is a very remarkable fact that most actors, when finding themselves in broad daylight, seemed, as it were, quite *dépaysés* and to have lost the actual remembrance of their exact poses and expression before the footlights, and I had often to quote the words to promote the attitudes.

'Charles Mathews was one day giving me a sitting at Regent Street in company with his charming wife, when I requested him to speak while the photograph was being taken. (It is well to notice that we had then neither dry plates nor instantaneous process; negatives were taken on collodion, and the sittings ranged from four to eight seconds, my system having always been to produce "half-tones", before any other photographic consideration. I am afraid the facilities now afforded by the mode of operating have been detrimental to the careful study of the "effects of light", which require for their production a constant modification of the time of exposure of the plate of film. "Instantaneous" is all very well as a facility for the operator, but it is certainly detrimental to the careful study of "Art in Photography", which too often seems reduced to a "mechanical trick". Pray excuse this digression from the subject, but I particularly wished to say that "speaking portraits" *cannot* be satisfactorily produced by the instantaneous process, for the simple reason that you mostly represent, then, *the mouth quite open*, while with a long exposure, you obtain the *resultante* of the expression of the mouth and features during the operation.) In compliance with my request Charles Mathews spoke, and as he said something funny his words brought a smile on Mrs Mathews' face – they were standing arm in arm – the speaking produced a double effect, the smile proving at the same time that he had been speaking.'

Camille Silvy was one of the first 'artistic' photographers; he gave his sitters elaborate and often beautiful backgrounds. His work is comparable with that of Cecil Beaton in modern times. Examples of Beau and Silvy are reproduced in this book among those of many of their colleagues of the '50s and '60s, including J. E. Mayall, who published *Celebrities of the London Stage*, theatrical character portraits with a biographical text in monthly parts early in the '60s; Herbert Watkins, a careful, straightforward portraitist; and Laroche, who has left many portraits and groups from Charles Kean's productions, and whose work is nearer to actual theatrical presentations than that of many of his colleagues.

Though still studio portraits, some of these early photographs portrayed the actors with actual props, and, on occasion, furniture from the stage production, though posed against painted drops. It was not till the '80s that new techniques made it possible for the camera to be taken into the theatre and on to the stage itself.

From the earliest days had been endeavours to take group pictures; a Daguerreotype of the Chartists on Kennington Common in 1848 has recently come to light. Until then the royal group at the opening of the Crystal Palace, at Sydenham in 1854, had been thought to be the earliest such picture; the interiors of the Great Exhibition in 1851 were unpeopled and taken with a long exposure.

In 1885, J. A. Smythe of Wimbledon registered for copyright purposes a number of photographs taken on stage by stage lighting. These include scenes from *The Mikado* produced in March 1885, and *Kenilworth* (a Burlesque) produced in December 1885. It is not till the end of the decade however that full sets, taken as it were, from a seat in the dress circle, began to appear. At first these seem to have been what we would now call 'set stills', records of the scenery, unpeopled; but soon, either by montage, or direct, full scenes began to appear as souvenirs reproduced in Collotype, or in magazines either in Woodburytype, or the now possible half-tone block, though they were still on occasion redrawn in line from magazine reproduction, but often stating that they were from the original photograph. The volumes of *The Theatre* which cover 1878 to 1897 are a valuable record of the changing techniques in photography and reproduction. We have included examples from 1889. Studio scenes, which were still reconstructed up to the 1900s, are easily identifiable.

In 1901, the editor of *The Photogram*, a prophetically named H. Snowden Ward, was writing for *The Playgoer* on 'Photography and the Footlights':

'In early Daguerreotype days, one was obliged to sit half an hour, in full sunlight and with whitened face, to secure a portrait. Now, a fraction of a second in good studio light is sufficient, and by some of the very latest developments of photography it is possible to actually snapshoot a performer on the stage with only the artificial light of a well-illuminated evening performance. This latest development is not by any means perfect, and the results obtained up to the present are not all that may be desired, but the mere possibility of the thing is marvellous. This is not the place for a technical description of how the thing is done; all available technical details have been given in *The Photogram* for September, 1901. Suffice to say that the new factor is a modified lens, invented by Dr Grun of Brighton, with which the exposure necessary under given conditions is greatly lessened.

'The shortening of exposure, by increasing the sensitiveness of photographic plates and the "rapidity" of Lenses, has been the one problem most constantly before photographic inventors, and in no field has it been more desirable than in theatrical photography. The reason for this will be seen anon.

'The portraying of professionals is, perhaps, even more truly than the photographing of babies, most pleasant, and yet most unsatisfactory.

'This arises from no fault of either party. The player is a good sitter because he (and still more she) can pose well, and can maintain a pose as long as is necessary. But so much of the charm of an actor depends upon colour, face-play, and the grace of motion, that posed portraits, incapable of representing these, are but travesties of the people they should portray. It is even now technically possible to photographically reproduce colour effects, and the kinetograph, which everybody knows, reproduces motion in a wonderful way. It is possible that some day, by the improvement of these methods, we may be able to reproduce colour and motion together, and by a method that shall not be too expensive. Meanwhile, and for the purpose of ordinary pictures and illustrations, photographers have endeavoured to suggest, rather than to reproduce, motion and colour-values. Wonderful results have been obtained in well-lighted studios by the patient co-operation of photographer and artiste; the photographer must be content to risk scores or even hundreds of failures.

'A great difficulty connected with the question of long exposure (though the connection is not at once apparent) is with the backgrounds and surroundings of the figures. Of course, the desirable thing is to be able to photograph figures and groups in their proper stage settings, with costumes, scenery and lighting as arranged by the artist of the stage picture, but the lights in the theatre, brilliant as they seem to the eye, are not photographically active enough to make a picture in any time that even the most stolid of players could maintain their pose and expression. Further, much of the scenery which looks so charming in the glow of light and colour, looks very flat and poor when translated into photographed black and white.

'To overcome this difficulty many photographers go to very great expense in providing in their own studios, backgrounds, accessories and furniture in keeping with the characters to be photographed. Obviously, this can only be done when a company's pictures are expected to be in great demand, and when some time can be allowed for the preparation of the scenery.

'However perfect may be the studio conditions there always remains the desirability of photographing on the stage itself, for large effects and tableaux, and here, again, photographers have spent immense ingenuity and much money. The result, nowadays, is simply a question of cost. If either the management, the illustrated press, or the public will reimburse the photographer for his outlay, he can produce wonderful effects by the lavish use of powerful electric lights in addition to the usual stage lighting. But this work cannot be done cheaply. In the case of a certain large London stage photographed not very long ago, the cost of wiring and fitting up the electric light was over £200, – no small sum for temporary fittings to be removed after a few hours' use. In this case the whole stage was fully lighted and photographed; an effort which will probably not be repeated until methods shall have been cheapened.

'Temporary electric lighting of a small portion of the stage, enough to provide for the photographing of a group of half a dozen or so figures, gets over many of the difficulties and reduces the cost enormously, and a modification of this method, which is ingenious in the extreme, has been very successfully applied by the London Stereoscopic Co. Arranging to light, say, one third of the whole stage at a time, they make three pictures of different parts of a great scene or tableau. An artist combines the three pictures, which thus become one, from which a new negative and any number of copies can be made. The photographers are willing and anxious to perfect their methods and extend their facilities, and there are many signs that players and managers wish to co-operate more and more fully with them.'

The search for instantaneous 'action' pictures and 'snap-shots' was both long and intermittently successful, and only reached its goal in comparatively recent times; though the one we have included of Farini, taken by Naudin of Brompton Road in the mid '60s, looks suspiciously like an 'action' picture. An illustrated magazine in 1909 published a photograph, which was then considered sensational, taken in Paris by Gerschel, of Nijinsky at the height of a leap; and at the end of the '20s, the *Morning Post* was exploiting the photographs of Armand Consol, taken during the actual performance, by stage lighting. Still by the final decade of the last century we can show outdoor scenes of entertainment and the comings and goings of actors and audiences.

The introduction of the picture postcard at the end of the century was soon recognised by publishers as a means of propagating the theatrical photograph. The earliest series (dated by postmark) that we have traced appears in 1902, and in the ensuing years, the craze reached unlooked-for proportions. The picture postcard beauty – the pin-up of her day – sold in thousands, making famous the work of a new generation of lady photographers like Lallie Garet-Charles and Lizzie Caswell-Smith; though their work was mainly off-stage and does not concern us in these pages, we have included some typical 'collective' cards and naturally some stage scenes come via the postcard.

After the work of the later stage photographers like Ellis and Walery, Downey, Bassano, and Window and Grove, there begin to creep in the impersonal grander-sounding or impressive 'business' names (foreshadowed earlier by the London Stereoscopic and Photographic Company, whose personnel remained anonymous). It becomes the era of the Dover Street Studios, The *Daily Mirror* Studios, Stage Photo Company or The Rotary Photographic Company (also one of the principal publishers of picture postcards, often catering exclusively for the theatre). They remained in vogue (with the possible exception of Foulsham and Banfield) until the return of the personalities which are out of our period. Post-last-war photographs at times have nothing of the feeling of a production or performance. Often little is left to recall for the future exactly what the production on the stage really was like; as H. Snowden Ward rightly supposes, it is up to the moneybags even more so today, and particularly what the press representative knows he can sell to the newspaper or magazine. This unfortunately dictates on what and how the managerial budget for photographs is spent.

EARLY VICTORIAN

5 *Hamlet* (Closet scene) from a stage box, 1857. The playbill
is for a performance at Drury Lane 16 April 1857 with
Charles Dillon and Mrs Weston. A photo-montage from a
hand-coloured stereoscopic slide

6 Charles Kean as Hamlet, 1858. From a hand coloured stereoscopic slide by Silvester Laroche. With the retirement of Macready in 1851, Charles Kean took his place as leader of the profession, and from 1850 to 1859 mounted spectacular productions of Shakespeare and other classics, interspersed with adaptations of French melodrama, at the Princess's Theatre

7 RIGHT Benjamin Webster as Robert Landry in *The Dead Heart* by Watts Phillips. A French Revolutionary drama at the Adelphi Theatre, 1859. Webster, an actor-manager and playwright, controlled both the Adelphi and Haymarket Theatres during the mid-Victorian era, both in partnership with Buckstone and Madame Céleste. (Photograph: Bauch and Bensley)

8 BELOW The Shadow Dance. Arranged by Oscar Byrne for Kean's production of *A Midsummer Night's Dream*, Princess's Theatre, 1856. Titania, Carlotta Leclercq, surrounded by her four attendants: Miss C. Adams, Miss B. Adams, Kate Terry and Miss Startin. From a hand coloured stereoscopic slide by Silvester Laroche

9 Samuel Phelps as Cardinal Wolsey in *Henry VIII*. (Photograph: J. E. Mayall, 1865.) Phelps took advantage of the breaking of the Theatres Royal monopoly in 1843 and became manager of Sadler's Wells Theatre, where he presented 34 of Shakespeare's plays among other classics. He continued to play his famous parts up to his death in 1878

10 John Baldwin Buckstone, comedian, manager and playwright, as Tony Lumpkin in *She Stoops to Conquer* at the Haymarket Theatre, 1856. (Photograph: Herbert Watkins.) Buckstone's management of the Haymarket Theatre spans the Victorian era, with many famous production and revivals including an Elizabethan staging of *The Taming of the Shrew* in 1844, 37 years before the experiments of William Poel

11 T. P. Cooke in 1853 as Long Tom Coffin in *The Pilot* by Edward Fitzball which he first played at the Adelphi Theatre in 1825. The many nautical dramas in which he acted gained him the name 'Sailor' Cooke. He created William in Douglas Jerrold's *Black-Eyed Susan* in 1829, and was still playing heroic British tars up to 1860 at the age of 74. (Photograph: J. E. Mayall)

12 Frederick Robson as Jem Baggs in *The Wandering Minstrel*, a farce by H. Mayhew Fitzroy, Olympic Theatre, 1853. (Photograph: Herbert Watkins.) 'The Great Little Robson' is singing 'Villikins and his Dinah' which he made famous. His short but brilliant career in farce and burlesque at the Olympic lasted from 1853 to 1864, when he died at the early age of 43, literally of stage fright

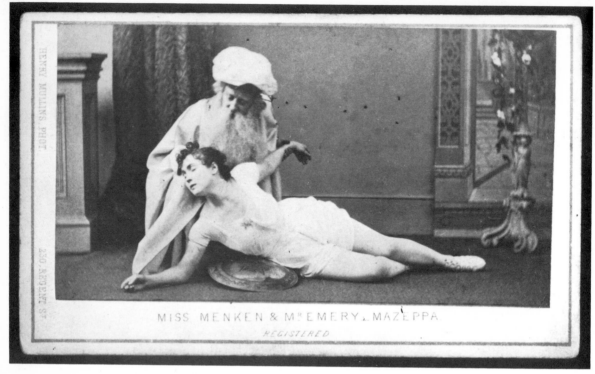

MISS MENKEN & Mr EMERY, MAZEPPA.
REGISTERED

13 ABOVE Adah Isaacs Menken and Sam Emery in *Mazeppa*, a Hippodramatic Spectacle at Astley's Amphitheatre, 1864. (Photograph: Henry Mullins.) This revival of H. M. Milner's adaptation of Byron's poem caused a sensation with Menken's supposed near-nude ride, strapped to the back of a horse

14 BELOW LEFT Charles J. Mathews as Dazzel in Boucicault's *London Assurance*, Haymarket Theatre, 1858. (Photograph: Herbert Watkins.) Mathews created the part in the original production at Covent Garden Theatre in 1841. He was considered the most brilliant light comedian of his generation right up till his death in 1878 at the age of 74

16 ABOVE Sophie Larkin, Marie Wilton and F. Young in *Ours* by T. W. Robertson, Prince of Wales's Theatre, 1866. (Photograph: Window and Bridge.) The 'cup and saucer' domestic dramas of Robertson, of which *Caste* is the most famous, mark a completely new era in naturalistic plays and productions. The management of the Bancrofts (Marie Wilton married Sidney 'Squire' Bancroft in 1867) lasted at this theatre until 1880, when they removed to the Haymarket Theatre until their retirement in 1885

15 LEFT John Clark and James Rodgers in *The Goose with the Golden Eggs*, a farce by Augustus Mayhew and Sutherland Edwards at the Strand Theatre, 1859. (Photograph: Camille Silvy.) This theatre became famous for its farces and burlesques throughout the period, and was a favourite haunt of the Prince of Wales

17 Henry Neville and Lydia Foote in *The Ticket-of-Leave Man*, Olympic Theatre, 1863. (Photograph: The London Stereoscopic and Photographic Company.) Tom Taylor's melodrama remained a stock piece for many years into the next century

18 ABOVE LEFT Emily Soldene as Drogan in Offenbach's *Geneviève de Brabant*, Philharmonic Theatre, Islington, 1871. (Photograph: Lafosse.) Soldene was the uncrowned queen of *opéra bouffe* on both sides of the Atlantic. It was these French delicacies, with their *travestie* roles, which dominated the musical stage until more or less swept aside by Gilbert and Sullivan

19 ABOVE Lydia Thompson, 1867. A famous actress and dancer in burlesque and *opéra bouffe*. With her husband Alexander Henderson she managed several West End theatres, and achieved great popularity. (Photograph: Camille Silvy)

20 LEFT J. L. Toole and Teresa Furtado in *Crying Jenny and Laughing Joan* by Offenbach, Adelphi Theatre, 1866. Toole, a low comedian both in farce and musical pieces, eventually opened his own theatre off the Strand in 1882, and lived to create Jasper Phipps in J. M. Barrie's first full-length play *Walker, London* in 1892, when he was 62. (Photograph: Adolphe Beau)

21 RIGHT Ellen Terry as Helen in *The Hunchback* by Sheridan Knowles, Olympic Theatre, 1866. The part of Helen was created by Fanny Kemble at Covent Garden in 1832, and the play long remained a stock piece. Ellen Terry, after her childhood appearances with Charles Kean, gained her experience in stock at Bath and Bristol. Following her disastrous marriage to Watts the painter, she returned to the London stage in 1866. (Photograph: Window and Bridge)

22 James Rogers as Eily O'Connor in *Little Eily O'Connor* by H. J. Byron, Strand Theatre, 1862. A burlesque of *The Colleen Bawn*, Boucicault's melodrama produced at the Adelphi in 1860. Throughout the Victorian era, no sooner was a play, an opera or even a ballet produced, than a burlesque version usually appeared – full of puns, with roles reversed and with topsyturvy topical plots. They were often the chance for a display of feminine limbs in the *travestie* roles. (Photograph: Southwell Brothers)

23 Fanny Josephs as Pekoe in *Aladdin; or, the Wonderful Scamp*, a burlesque by H. J. Byron, Strand Theatre, 1861. (Photograph: Charles F. Gladwell.) The burlesqueing of fairy-tale plots, which were later to become associated with pantomime, and the *travestie* tradition, has led to much confusion as to which was which. Pantomime, as we came to know it, drew its 'boys' and 'dames' from burlesque, and its artists and songs from the music halls and *opéra bouffe*. Augustus Harris fused the two worlds at Drury Lane in the early 1880s

24 Charlotte Saunders as William Tell in *Tell, and the Strike of the Cantons; or, the Pair, the Meddler, and the Apple*. A Fairy Extravaganza by Francis Talfourd, Strand Theatre, 1859. The differences between Burlesque and Extravaganza are subtle. Grove describes the latter as 'Any work of art, in which accepted forms are caricatured, and recognised laws violated, with a purpose' – which would seem to apply to Burlesque too! However, contemporary authors carefully differentiated between the two on their playbills. (Photograph: Camille Silvy)

25 Henry Irving as Mathias in *The Bells*, Leopold Lewis's adaptation from the French, Lyceum Theatre, 1871. Irving made his sensational appearance in *The Bells* under the Bateman management, but by 1878 was in full control of the theatre with Ellen Terry as his leading lady. They dominated the London theatre till the end of the century. In 1895 Irving became the first actor to receive a knighthood, at last making the rogues and vagabonds of the theatre into respectable citizens! (Photograph: The London Stereoscopic and Photographic Company)

26 RIGHT W. H. Kendal and his wife Madge Robertson in *Diplomacy* by B. C. Stephenson and Clement Scott (from the French), Prince of Wales's Theatre. 1878. This was produced under the Bankroft management and many times revived. The Kendals, with John Hare, were to move into the management of the St James's Theatre; and later, on his own, Hare went to the Royal Court. (Photograph: Window and Grove)

28 BELOW *Olivia*, W. G. Wills stage version of Goldsmith's *The Vicar of Wakefield*, at the Royal Court Theatre, 1878. The full company. (Photograph: Elliott and Fry.) Under Hare's management, Herman Vezin created the Vicar (a part later to be played by Irving at the Lyceum) with Ellen Terry at his feet, the baby Gordon Craig on his knee, and Edith Craig by his side. (Ellen Terry's children by E. W. Godwin)

27 ABOVE The Bancrofts retire, 20 July 1885; a farewell Souvenir photograph by Window and Grove. After their years of management at the Prince of Wales's, the St James's and the Haymarket Theatres they retired in Royal glory. Sir Squire Bancroft, when he died in 1926, left over £175,000, an estate only surpassed by that of his fellow actor-manager Sir Charles Wyndham, as the largest theatrical fortune of the Victorian and Edwardian era

29 ABOVE LEFT Giuseppe Mario as Faust in Gounod's opera, Covent Garden, 1864. *Faust* was first heard in London in a concert version at the Canterbury, the Lambeth music hall. It reached the stage at Her Majesty's in 1863, and Covent Garden a year later, with Patti as Marguerite. Mario had been the *beau idéal* tenor since 1838. (Photograph: L. Caldesi and Co.)

30 ABOVE Giulia Grisi as Norma in Bellini's opera, which she first sang at Her Majesty's in 1837. With her husband Mario, she moved to Covent Garden when it became The Royal Italian Opera in 1847. She was still singing the part in 1861 when she retired

31 LEFT Marietta Alboni in *Marta*, Her Majesty's Theatre, 1860. Marietta was the contralto who often sang with Mario and Grisi at Her Majesty's and followed them to Covent Garden, but soon returned to Her Majesty's, where she sang for many years

32 RIGHT Adelina Patti as Juliet in Gounod's opera, 1880s. From her London début in 1861, until the advent of Melba in 1888, she remained at Covent Garden, the undisputed 'Queen of Song'. (Photograph: The London Stereoscopic and Photographic Company)

33 RIGHT 'Ballet dancers in the Green Room.' A stereoscopic slide of the mid-1860s

34 LEFT Sara Wright, 'Wiry Sal', also known as 'Sara the Kicker'. She caused a sensation when she appeared with the Colona Troupe, who introduced the Can Can (The Parisienne Quadrille) in 1870. She later went to America, Australia and New Zealand. This photograph by Bradley and Rulofson was taken in San Francisco in 1877, when she was on tour with Emily Soldene's company

35 RIGHT Giovannina Pitteri as The Star of Hope in *The Demon's Bride*, Alhambra Theatre, 1874. Choreography by Dewinne, with music by Jacobi. This was typical of the ballets which followed the decline of 'The Romantic Ballet', and remained in vogue at the Alhambra and the Empire until the Russian invasion of the early 1900s

36 ABOVE A montage group of artists who performed at the Birmingham Music Festival, 1867. Festivals were part of the musical world all through the Victorian era. The great new industrial towns such as Liverpool, Birmingham and Leeds, built vast halls to house their festivals, and brought great singers, musicians, conductors and composers to their concerts. This group includes Julius Benedict, Teresa Tietjens, Christine Nilsson, Mme Lemens-Sherrington, Mme Stainton-Dolby, Patey-Whytlock, Cummings, Weiss, Stimson (at the piano), Arabella Goddard, Charles Santley, Sims Reeves, Sterndale Bennett, Michael Costa and Belletti. (Photograph: H. J. Whitlock)

37 LEFT The London Pavilion, Tichborne Street. This first 'Music Hall de Luxe' grew in 1861 from the roofed-in stableyard of The Black Horse Coaching Inn. Music Halls derived from the Catch and Glee clubs of London taverns and by the 1850s, the publicans began to convert their large rooms into music halls, complete with a chairman, often mine host himself. These halls mainly catered for a mixed working-class population on the fringes of central London. In the West End, the more musical and sophisticated Song and Supper Rooms were frequented by a Bohemian all-male audience

39 RIGHT Sam Cowell as The Railway Porter – a typical comedian who worked between Song and Supper Rooms and Music Halls and achieved great popularity on both sides of the Atlantic before his early death in 1864.

38 BELOW Deacon's Music Hall, Islington, opposite Sadler's Wells, photographed before demolition in 1891, shows clearly the addition of a hall to the tavern. This was to give way to the grandiose buildings of the mid-1880s, when Music Halls became firmly established

40 The Great Exhibition of 1851: the Eastern Nave. The idea of an Exhibition of the Arts and Industries of All Nations was conceived by the Prince Consort and a great 'Crystal Palace' of iron and glass to house it was designed by Joseph Paxton and arose in Hyde Park. (Photograph: H. Owen and M. Farrier)

41 RIGHT The Crystal Palace, Sydenham, 1855. When the Great Exhibition finished in 1851, the building was moved to the top of Sydenham Hill in Kent, and reassembled with additions including the towers. It was opened by Queen Victoria and Prince Albert in 1853, and became the centre for exhibitions, concerts, and firework displays, and an arts centre for South London, until it was burnt to the ground in 1936. (Photograph: Philip Henry Delamotte)

42 BELOW The Handel Festivals at The Crystal Palace were a regular event for many years and part of the London musical scene. A vast orchestra, organ and chorus performed the oratorios to enthusiastic audiences. A souvenir *carte de visite* by the official photographers to the Palace, Negretti and Zambra

CRYSTAL PALACE
TRIENNIAL HANDEL FESTIVAL.

FOUR THOUSAND PERFORMERS.
Costuzie - Mr Costa.

VIEW OF ORCHESTRA.

Rehearsal, Friday, June 23rd.
Messiah, Monday, June 26th.

Selection, Wednesday, June 28th.
Israel, Friday, June 30th.

1865.

Negretti and Zambra, Photographers to the Crystal Palace.

44 General Mite, a successor to Tom Thumb in the 1880s. 'General Mite; 17 years old, weighs nine pounds. He is bright, smart and intelligent, and a perfect man in miniature.' (Photograph: Brown, Barnes and Bell)

43 Phineas T. Barnum, Prince of Humbugs, with General Tom Thumb. The great American showman first brought Tom Thumb to London in 1844. His visit to Queen Victoria and Prince Albert at Buckingham Palace set the seal on his success, and he returned several times to this country. The Victorians had great enthusiasm for freaks and extraordinary characters which were often on display at the Egyptian Hall in Piccadilly

45 Chang-Yu-Sing, the Chinese Giant. He came to London in 1865, aged 19 and 7 ft 9 in tall. He achieved presentation to the Prince of Wales, and was seen at the Egyptian Hall in company with other 'Celestials'. (Photograph: A. Bogardus, New York)

46 Marian the Giantess was '8 ft 2 in in height and still growing, when only 16 years old'. She appeared on the stage at the Alhambra in *Babel and Bijou* in 1882, as well as exhibiting herself up and down the country. (Photograph: James Bacon, Newcastle-upon-Tyne)

47 ABOVE LEFT The Chinese Dwarf, who held levées with the Chinese Giant at the Egyptian Hall, 1865. (Photograph: The London Stereoscopic and Photographic Company)

48 LEFT 'The Fair Circassian', exhibited at the Egyptian Hall at the same time as the original Siamese twins in 1859. (Photograph: Wilson and Beadell.) 'The Circassian, Zobeide Luti by name, was rescued, at four years of age, from a slave dealer, and was educated by her preserver, an Austrian nobleman. Such is the account given of this lady, who is very handsome and has a profusion of strong and vigorous brown hair, not in long tresses, but standing out in a mass from her head. The "Circassian" speaks five languages, and anyone is at liberty to test her skill as a linguist. She is dressed in a robe of brown satin, and wears Turkish unmentionables of the same material. Zobeide Luti is dark in complexion, and her receipts from selling her portrait must be something considerable'

49 LEFT 'The Two-headed Nightingale', shown in London in the 1870s. The original Siamese twins, Chang and Eng, caused a sensation on both sides of the Atlantic and had several successors to whom they gave the name of 'Siamese twins'

50 RIGHT Blondin (Jean François Gravelet), who achieved world fame in 1859 by crossing Niagara Falls on a tight-rope with a wheelbarrow, and returning with a man on his back. He came to London in 1861 and performed similar feats, crossing the central transept of the Crystal Palace on a number of occasions. A photo-montage by Negretti and Zambra, official photographers to Crystal Palace

51 Mlle Victoria, 'Queen on the Lofty Wire'. The sensation of Blondin's exploits encouraged many imitators, including 'The Female Blondin' (Madame Geneviève: her real name was Selina Young) who attempted to cross the Thames from Battersea to Cremorne Gardens on a tight-rope in 1861. One suspects that many of the so-called 'sensational females' were in fact young boys, as in the case of Mlle Ella, 'a fair Equestrienne' who appeared at Drury Lane in the late 1850s with an American circus

52 LEFT El Nino Farini, performing on the trapeze as a child. An early action photograph by Naudin, in the mid 1860s. One of the Farini troupe who often performed at Cremorne Gardens. When he grew up, he was re-introduced by his father as Mlle Lulu, 'The beautiful Circassian Gymnast', at the Royal Amphitheatre, Holborn in 1871, when 'she' was shot out of a cannon. A visit by the Prince and Princess of Wales caused humanitarians and moralists to protest at the danger to the 'young lady', only to be confounded when it was proved that she was 'a lubly boy'

53 Léotard, 'The daring young man on the flying trapeze', 1861. His appearances at the Alhambra over the heads of the audiences were sensational. He gave his name to the costume, and the song sung by George Leybourne gave him immortality. (Photograph: Disderi, Paris)

54 Zazel (Rosa Star), 'The Human Cannon Ball'. Another creation of old Farini, the showman at the Royal Aquarium, Westminster in 1877. As with Lulu and later Zaeo, a trapeze artist, moralists were aroused by both the feats and the publicity: posters were banned as being indecent at the demand of 'The Central Vigilance Society for the Repression of Immorality', but the popularity of both ladies lasted at the Aquarium well into the 1890s. (Photograph: London Stereoscopic and Photographic Company)

55 John Parry as himself and in *A Peculiar Family* at the Gallery of Illustration, 1865. Double and triple portraits had a vogue in the 1860s when photographers exploited the possibilities of trick photography. Parry had been a solo entertainer at the piano for many years when he joined the German Reeds in their early days in sketches and light operas. (From a Binograph by McLean and Haes)

56 Frederic Macabe, the ventriloquist, mimic, and musician as Miss May and as The Lancashire Lad in one of his Entertainments. A solo entertainer in the Charles Mathews tradition, he attracted audiences to concert halls and town halls up and down the country. (A Binograph by Walker and Sons, 1860s)

57 Mr and Mrs German Reed in a sketch in the late 1850s. From a stereoscopic slide. Thomas German Reed and his wife Priscilla Horton established themselves at the Royal Gallery of Illustration in Waterloo Place, Lower Regent Street in 1856 with a polite musical 'Entertainment', suitable for a middle-class and family audience who would not go to the music hall, or even the theatre (except for pantomime) let alone the French comic opera performances, which attracted a Bohemian audience! They became extremely popular and moved to the St George's Hall in 1867. They staged early works by Gilbert and by Sullivan (who were not yet in collaboration) and their traditional 'Entertainment' lasted until 1895. Nearly all the solo entertainers of the period appeared under their banner

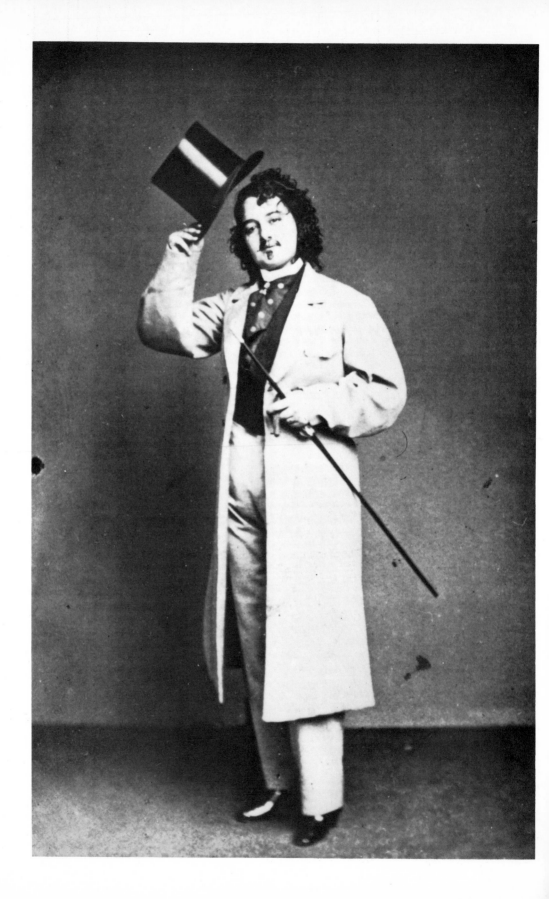

58 LEFT Mrs Howard Paul in *Home and Abroad*. With her husband she presented an entertainment throughout the 1860s, similar to that of the German Reeds. Most of these entertainers used *travestie* as an integral part of their work, following the current burlesque fashion. (Photograph: Alexander Bassano, *c.* 1863)

59 William Love, the Dramatic Polyphonist, as Miss Meddler in his 'Ventriloquial Entertainment', 1855. Love's one-man performance had 'totalled 200 nights at the Royal Gallery and 2,360 in London', by 1855. He continued to add to this until his death in 1867. (From a stereoscopic slide)

60 Charles Dickens gave the first public reading from his works at the St Martin's Hall, Long Acre in 1858, and continued to do so with great success until his death in 1870. (From a stereoscopic slide by Herbert Watkins, 1859)

61 'The Green Room on the occasion of the Amateur
Performance of *A Wolf in Sheep's Clothing* and *Cox and Box*,
in aid of the Benefit Fund', Adelphi Theatre, 11 May 1867.
(Photograph: The London Stereoscopic and Photographic
Company.) The group includes professional and literary
figures, who banded together to raise money for the widow
of Charles H. Bennett, the children's writer. *Cox and Box*
by Arthur Sullivan and F. C. Burnand was given its first
performance at this matinee. The group includes: Robert
Pritchett, Shirley Brooks, Arthur J. Lewis, Mark Lemon,
Quintin Twiss, John Tenniel, Arthur Blunt (Cecil) and
Henry Silver; and (bottom row) Arthur Sullivan, Ellen
Terry, George du Maurier, Kate Terry and Tom Taylor.
Charity performances and benefits by amateur actors of the
literary and Bohemian world were frequent, Charles
Dickens and W. S. Gilbert often taking part

62 'The *Bal Masqué*' from a stereoscopic slide of the late
1850s. Masked and fancy dress balls were popular in the
early Victorian period, and even Queen Victoria and Prince
Albert indulged in this pastime at Buckingham Palace

LATE VICTORIAN

63 *A man's Shadow* by Robert Buchanan (from the French).
Beerbohm Tree and Company, Haymarket Theatre, 1889.
An early full-stage photograph by Herbert Barraud. This is
possibly a montage, but by the end of the '80s, it had
become possible to photograph productions actually on
stage

64 William Terriss and Jessie Millward in *The Harbour
Lights* by George R. Sims and Henry Pettitt. Adelphi
Theatre, 1885. An 'Adelphi drama' which was typical of
the many which starred 'Breezy Bill' Terriss, up to his
murder in 1897 at his private entrance to the theatre in
Maiden Lane. (Photograph: Window and Grove)

65 Ellaline Terriss, Lily Hanbury and Pattie Browne in *The Amazons*, a farcical romance by A. W. Pinero, Royal Court Theatre, 1893. The New Woman was beginning to emerge, but Pinero's play about these young ladies brought up as boys by an eccentric mother, pointed a moral when love came their way. (Photograph: Alfred Ellis)

66 Kate Rorke and Johnstone Forbes-Robertson in *Lady Bountiful* by A. W. Pinero, Garrick Theatre, 1891. 'I've come back to England thinking to discharge a debt. Be Lady Bountiful to me still and take the remaining years of my life for it.' (Photograph: The London Stereoscopic Company)

67 ABOVE *The Idler* by C. Haddon Chambers. George Alexander and Company on the stage of the St James's Theatre, 1891. A photograph by Alfred Ellis issued as a souvenir

68 RIGHT, ABOVE George Alexander and Mrs Patrick Campbell in *The Second Mrs Tanqueray* by A. W. Pinero, St James's Theatre, 1893. The St James's became the home of plays dealing with society's problems and taboos, reflecting 'Our Parish of St James's'. (Photograph: Alfred Ellis)

69 *Lady Windermere's Fan* by Oscar Wilde, St James's Theatre, 1892. 'What's the difference between scandal and gossip?' Left to right: Ben Webster, A. Vane-Tempest, Nutcombe Gould, H. H. Vincent and George Alexander. This was Wilde's first theatrical success: Alexander was also to stage *The Importance of Being Earnest* in 1895, which was running when the Wilde scandal broke. (Photograph: Alfred Ellis)

70 The Forum Scene, *Julius Caesar*, Her Majesty's Theatre, 1898. Tree's spectacular productions of Shakespeare became a byword when he moved from the Haymarket to this theatre he built on the site of the old Opera House in 1897. (Photograph: The London Stereoscopic Company)

71 Herbert Beerbohm Tree and Mrs Patrick Campbell in *John-A-Dreams* by C. Haddon Chambers, Haymarket Theatre, 1894. A photograph by J. C. Turner and Company's Electric Light Studio. Tree for once was seen without a heavy disguise, and in a contemporary play; it was partly set on 'The Deck of the Yacht *Moonbeam* at Anchor in Southampton Water'

72 *Measure for Measure*: William Poel's production at the Royalty Theatre, 1893, with himself as Angelo. Poel's experimental productions of Shakespeare, without cuts and with continuous action on an Elizabethan-style stage, started with a production of the First Quarto *Hamlet* in the St George's Hall in 1881. He founded the Elizabethan Stage Society in 1895. It was from these experiments that the great Shakespearean directors of the next generation drew their inspiration, including Granville Barker and Iden Payne. (Photograph: Russell and Sons)

73 The Queen and Ophelia in an all-male production by Poel of *Hamlet*. Poel started his campaign with amateurs, only employing professionals later in his work. At times he used all-male casts in the Elizabethan manner

74 ABOVE Martin Harvey and Grace Warner in *The Only Way*, Freeman Wills' and Frederick Langbridge's adaptation of Dickens's *A Tale of Two Cities*, Lyceum Theatre, 1899. This play drew audiences on tour all over the country for a generation. It had ten revivals in London alone and Harvey was playing Sidney Carton almost up to his death in 1944. The longevity of their productions was a feature of the later Victorian and Edwardian actor-managers. (Photograph: The London Stereoscopic Company)

75 LEFT Charles Wyndham and Mary Moore in *David Garrick*, T. W. Robertson's adaptation of a French play (which had nothing at all to do with the great English actor!). It was first produced with Edward Sothern in 1864. Wyndham made the part his own, with Mary Moore (whom he later married) as his leading lady in 1886 at the Criterion Theatre. They were still playing the roles in 1902. (Photograph: Herbert Barraud)

77 RIGHT *Mamma!*, a farcical comedy by Sydney Grundy (from the French), Criterion Theatre, 1901. A revival of an '80s play typical of the farces of the period. The company is Mrs Calvert, Ethel Mathews, George Giddens and Nellie Sydney. (Photograph: Alfred Ellis and Walery)

76 ABOVE *Charley's Aunt* by Brandon Thomas, Royalty Theatre, 1892. W. S. Penley created the part of Lord Fancourt Babberley, which has remained the pet of comedians up to the present day. (Photograph: J. C. Turner and Co.)

78 ABOVE Lillie Langtry in *Princess George* by Charles Coghlan (from the French), Prince of Wales' Theatre, 1885. From a photograph by James Lafayette, Dublin, a Royal photographer of his day. Mrs Langtry arrived in London, first as a Society beauty, 'The Jersey Lily', and later exhibited herself on the stage as an actress for charity, though soon becoming a professional and established actress-manager on both sides of the Atlantic. Her liaison with the Prince of Wales contributed much to her success and notoriety

79 LEFT *The Mikado*, Savoy Theatre, 1885. 'The Three Little Maids': Sybil Grey, Leonora Braham and Jessie Bond. Gilbert and Sullivan, with the managerial assistance of D'Oyly Carte, reformed the musical stage, banishing all French 'naughtiness' and making it a suitable entertainment for both Society and the middle classes. Of their 14 collaborations *The Mikado* remains the most successful and world-famous, its original run of 672 performances being the longest of the series. (Photograph: Herbert Barraud)

80 Nellie Farren in *Ruy Blas and The Blasé Roué*, a Gaiety Theatre Burlesque, 1889. The illness and retirement of Nellie Farren in 1891 marked the virtual death of Burlesque, and before her Farewell Benefit at Drury Lane in 1898, George Edwardes had 'invented' Musical Comedy. (Photograph: The London Stereoscopic Company)

81 'The Foundlings', *The Shop Girl*, Gaiety Theatre, 1894. The famous 'Gaiety Girls' were a creation of George Edwardes when he presented the first musical comedy *A Gaiety Girl* at the Prince of Wales' Theatre in 1893. For the first time, the company was dressed in *couture* clothes, and the plot was contemporary. A new era had begun. (Photograph: Alfred Ellis)

82 The Royal Opera House, Covent Garden, 'dressed over all' for the Diamond Jubilee Gala, 1897. Built in 1858, it has become one of the premier opera houses of the world, the scene of many Galas the Royal visits and the home of 'The Golden Age of Opera'

83 Emma Albani as Marguerite in *Faust*, Covent Garden, 1875. A French-Canadian soprano who made her début at The Garden in 1872, Emma wisely married Ernest Gye, the son of the impresario who had rebuilt the theatre after the great fire of 1856. She remained a great favourite for the next generation. (Photograph: The London Stereoscopic and Photographic Company)

84 Edouard de Reszke as Mephistopheles in *Faust* which he first performed at Covent Garden in 1884. (Photograph: Aimé Dupont)

85 BELOW LEFT Jean de Reszke as Lohengrin in Wagner's opera at Covent Garden, where he first sang the part in 1888. For many years opera was sung in Italian only. Covent Garden was in fact known as The Royal Italian Opera, but, by the turn of the century, German was allowed! 'De Reszke nights' with Jean and his brother Edouard, often with Melba, became the highlights of the season (Photograph Aimé Dupont, New York)

86 Nellie Melba and Fernando de Lucia in *I Pagliacci*, Covent Garden, 1893. The first London performance of Leoncavallo's opera. (Photograph: Alfred Ellis)

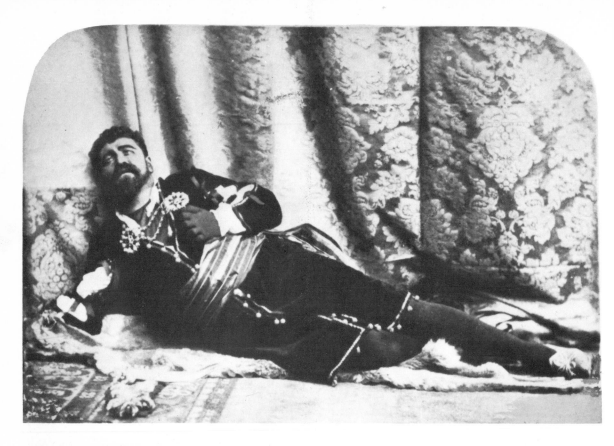

87 Francesco Tamagno as Otello in Verdi's opera, the title role of which he created in 1887 at La Scala, and sang two years later at the Lyceum Theatre (Photograph: R. J. Falk, New York, 1890)

88 Emma Calvé as Santuzza in *Cavalleria Rustican*, Covent Garden, 1892. She sang the part opposite de Lucia. This opera and *I Pagliacci* became the inseparable twins they still remain. (Photograph: Alexander Bassano)

89 'Mrs Brown Potter amuses herself with the Gramophone'. By the turn of the century, the gramophone (which had been invented in 1877) was becoming recognised as a means of entertaining, and great singers were soon allowing their voices to be preserved for posterity. (Photograph: Foulsham and Banfield, 1902)

90 'Listening to the Electrophone', 1899. 'A picturesque and entertaining adjunct to the London Telephone system', the Electrophone connected subscribers to 'Theatres, Music Halls, Concert Halls and Places of Worship, etc., switched on at Home and heard to perfection'. A listening studio was also provided at their Gerrard Street offices

91 The Empire, Leeds, 1898, a typical example of the music halls designed by Frank Matcham up and down the country. The giant syndicates of Moss, Stoll and other provincial magnates provided entertainments for the masses in 'The Golden Age of Music Hall'.

92 Vesta Tilley, 'The London Idol'. An 1880s' photograph of the great male impersonator before she adopted complete male attire. She is here following the tradition of Nellie Power using essential props with the typical burlesque costume of the day. (Photograph: Symonds and Co., Portsmouth)

93 Lottie Collins singing 'Ta-ra-ra-Boom-de-ay', 1891. The song, and its Can Can like dance which has become the epitome of the 'naughty nineties', was an English adaptation of an American original. Lottie Collins introduced it into pantomime when she played Alice Fitzwarren in *Dick Whittington* at the Grand Theatre, Islington. So great was its success that she was asked to repeat it at the Gaiety Theatre in the burlesque *Cinder-Ellen-Up-Too-Late*. (Photograph: Russell and Sons)

94 Ada Reeve singing 'That Little Word Yes', 1891. Starting her career in pantomime and melodrama, she became a child star of the halls on both sides of the Atlantic. She refused the blandishments of George Edwardes to succeed Nellie Farren at the Gaiety, waiting to become its first musical comedy leading lady in *The Shop Girl* in 1894. (Photograph: London Stereoscopic Company)

96 George Robey, 'The Prime Minister of Mirth', singing 'The Tramp', 1899. One of the greatest of music hall comedians, soon after his début as a trial turn in 1891, he 'found' the mock clergyman's coat and large eyebrows, which were to become his trade-mark for the rest of his career

95 Charles Coborn singing 'The Man Who Broke the Bank at Monte Carlo', 1894. It was this song and 'Two Lovely Black Eyes' (1886) which made the career of Coborn, a typical comedian, and took him to the top of the bill, where he remained for the rest of his life

98 Dan Leno as 'The Shop Walker' or 'Walk This Way –
Step This Way', 1892. The greatest of all comedians: his
performances by Royal Command earned him the title of
'The King's Jester'. His career was short, but he left behind
a legend when he died at only 43 in 1904. (Photograph:
Langfier)

97 Albert Chevalier singing 'The Coster's Serenade', 1891.
Originally a straight actor, he went on the halls with songs
and monologues of his own writing, with music by his
brother-in-law Charles Ingle. His coster studies, including
'My Old Dutch' and 'Wot Cher' or 'Knocked 'em in the Old
Kent Road', earned him the title of 'The Coster Laureate'.
(Photograph: The London Stereoscopic Company)

99 Marie Lloyd as Principle Boy in pantomime (late '90s). One of the greatest comediennes of the halls, her saucy songs, with their wink and innuendo, became famous. As did many of her contemporaries, she appeared in pantomime at Christmas, attracting an audience which never would have dared to venture to see her at the 'wicked' music halls. (Photograph: Hana)

100 Herbert Campbell as Eliza the Cook and Dan Leno as Idle Jack in *Dick Whittington*, Drury lane, 1894. The 'New Woman' and a Guardsman came in for burlesque in the typical pantomime tradition. Leno and Campbell were a partnership in pantomimes which lasted at the Lane from 1888 until they both died in 1904 (Photograph: Hana)

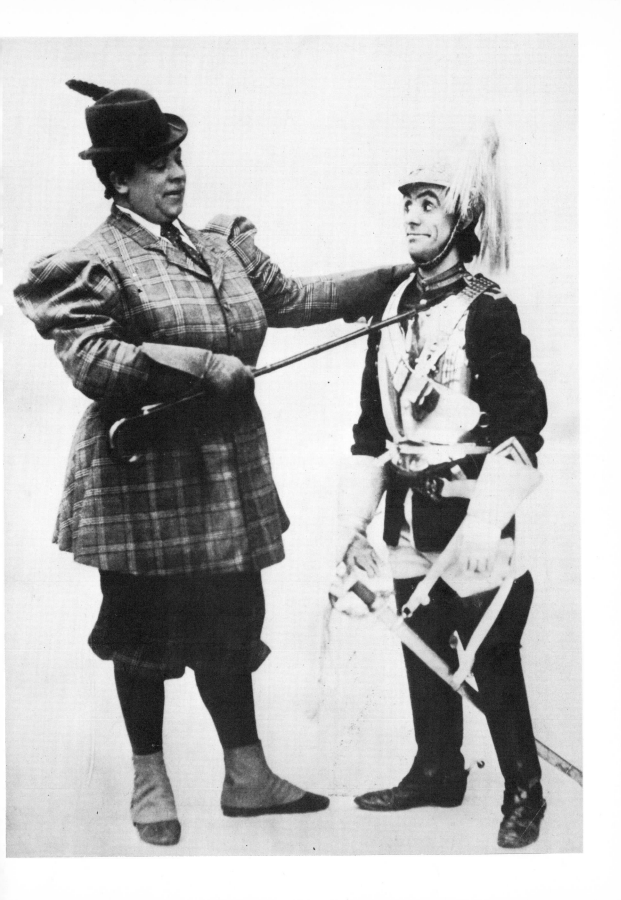

101 The Egyptian Hall, Piccadilly at the turn of the century. Opened in 1812, originally as Bullock's Museum and an exhibition hall, it became the home of Maskelyn and Cooke's Magical Entertainments in 1873. All the great magicians of the age appeared under their banner until the hall was demolished in 1904. John Maskelyn then moved, with a new partner, David Devant, to the St George's Hall in Langham Place, where 'Maskelyn's Mysteries' remained firmly established until 1933. Maskelyn was one of the pioneer exhibitors of the newly-invented animated pictures, which began to be shown in public in 1896

102 Charles Bertram and Mlle Patrice performing 'The Vanishing Lady' at the Egyptian Hall, 1886. The famous illusion was perfected in Paris by a French magician, De Kolta, as 'L'escamotage en personne vivant', but was given in London, by special permission, by Charles Bertram, when he became the Prince of Wales' favourite conjurer. (Photograph: The London Stereoscopic and Photographic Company)

103 George Grossmith, the piano entertainer, 1890. The second George Grossmith (his father George was a lecturer) was the first star comedian of the Gilbert and Sullivan operas when he joined the company in 1878. He remained with them until 1889, when he returned to his original one-man entertainment with songs at the piano, a side of his career which he had never completely abandoned. His son, also George, became the famous Gaiety comedian of Edwardian days. (Photograph: Alfred Ellis)

104 The Mohawk, Moore and Burgess Minstrels at the St James's Hall, 1901. Minstrelsy became established in the small St James's Hall (the large hall upstairs was a famous concert room) where The Christy Minstrels first appeared in 1859. Various other companies were formed, and either disbanded or merged. The final company was formed by Moore and Burgess, who remained at the hall, joined by The Mohawk's Company from the Agricultural Hall, Islington. The company survived until 1904 when the hall was closed and a much-loved popular entertainment passed from the London scene

105 *The Merry Wives of Windsor* as performed by the
Oxford University Dramatic Society, 1896. The scenery for
this production was specially designed by E. H. Clark, MA
(New College) and E. R. Jones (who painted all the sets).
The costumes came from Beerbohm Tree's wardrobe, and
Sullivan allowed his incidental music in manuscript to be
used for the last act. The production was directed by
George R. Foss. Of the ladies who were co-opted for the
cast, Lilian Braithwaite played Ann Page. (Photograph:
Hills and Saunders, Oxford.) The O.U.D.S. was formed in
1883 to perform in public in spite of much difficulty during
preceding years with the College authorities, who had
virtually banned dramatic entertainment since the '70s.
Even when at last allowed, ladies had to be brought in (if
professional) as no female impersonation was permitted (as
at Cambridge). The early days were famous for the
members who later joined 'the profession', Arthur
Bourchier and H. B. Irving being amongst them. These
amateur performances became a traditional trying-out
ground for the next few generations. At Cambridge the
A.D.C. and the Marlowe Society long continued the 'drag'
tradition

106 Alex Armstein (and assistants), 'Late Musical Director
to Mr John Hare, Garrick Theatre'. Anthenaeum Hall,
Brighton 1893, and 'On the Promenade Season 1894'

107 Dancing to a street organ, London, 1900

108 Punch and Judy on the sands at Ilfracombe in the '90s

109 Punch and Judy in a London square, 1900. As at Ilfracombe, 'By Royal Appointment'!

110 Ginett's Circus comes to Chichester in the '90s

111 A dancing bear, Buttermarket, Bury St Edmunds, 1900

112 The Fat Lady, a traditional side-show at country fairs.
A '90s' photograph by W. Stringer, Liverpool

113 Sequah, the Medicine Man. A '90s' photograph by W.
Eskett, Lendal, York. The ageless quack doctor and
mountebank, a survival from the sixteenth century at
country fairs

114 Listening to the band in Hyde Park, 1900

115 Singing to patients at The London Hospital, 1900

116 ABOVE Wilma Norman Neruda (Lady Hallé). A German violinist, who married Sir Charles Hallé, founder and conductor of the Hallé Orchestra at the Free Trade Hall, Manchester. (Photograph: Alexander Bassano, 1885)

117 ABOVE RIGHT Joseph Joachim, the German violinist and composer, a great favourite at the Monday Popular Concerts at the Crystal Palace in the '80s. (Photograph: Alexander Bassano)

118 Ignace Jan Paderewski, the Polish pianist whose romantic appeal added greatly to his popularity when he first came to London in 1890. He remained a part of the musical world for many years and lived on to become the first President of liberated Poland after the Great War

EDWARDIAN

121 *Peter Pan* by J. M. Barrie, Duke of York's Theatre, 1904. (Photograph: Ellis and Walery.) Nina Boucicault, the first Peter, with Hilda Trevelyan as Wendy, and Gerald du Maurier as Hook. Although not intended as a Christmas attraction it has been revived annually, with only a few exceptions

119 OPPOSITE, ABOVE *You Never Can Tell* by George Bernard Shaw, Royal Court Theatre, 1906. (Photograph: The Dover Street Studios.) The Vedrenne-Barker seasons at the Royal Court placed Shaw firmly in front of the London playgoer. Written in 1896, *You Never Can Tell* had its first run of ten weeks in 1906. The 'New Drama', which had slowly emerged from the play-producing societies, had begun to make its mark

120 OPPOSITE, BELOW *Lady Frederick* by W. Somerset Maugham, Royal Court Theatre, 1907. (Photograph: The Dover Street Studios.) Lord Meneston (Graham Browne) learns the secret of Lady Frederick's (Ethel Irving) beauty. This was Maugham's sixth play, but his first success; during its run of 422 performances he had three other plays produced

122 RIGHT *The Walls of Jericho* by Alfred Sutro, Garrick Theatre, 1904. The young wife (Violet Vanbrugh) and her fast ways disgust her husband from Australia (Arthur Bourchier). 'The Smart Set Whipped' by a topical dramatist. (Photograph: Ellis and Walery)

123 *The Winter's Tale*. The Benson Company at the Shakespeare Memorial Theatre, Stratford-upon-Avon, 1903. Ada Farrar as Hermione, Frank Benson as Leontes, and Ethel Dane as Mamillius. The Benson Company ruled the Festivals at Stratford from 1886 till 1916 and in between toured the provinces with Benson's particular brand of Shakespeare. (Photograph: Ellis and Walery)

124 Constance and Frank Benson in *Macbeth*, Stratford-upon-Avon, 1903. 'Ma' and 'Pa' Benson provided a cradle for the next generation of Shakespearean actors (Photograph: Ellis and Walery)

125 ABOVE *Between Two Women* by Frederick Melville, Terriss's, Rotherhithe, 1902. The Melville Brothers wrote countless melodramas which toured, and eventually found a London home under their management at the Lyceum Theatre from 1909

126 LEFT *Life's Sweetest Sins* by W. A. Brabner, Theatre Royal, Stratford East, London, 1905. Touring melodrama often advertised itself by postcard throw-aways, in no mean terms proclaiming their wares. Black was black, and white was white: melodrama held sway until supplanted by the cinema as the drama of the masses.

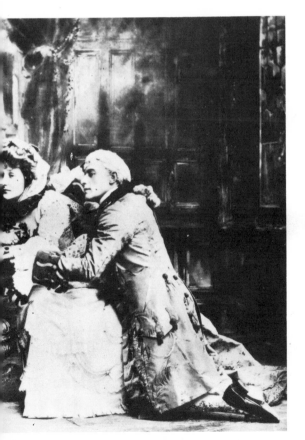

127 ABOVE *The Whip* by Cecil Raleigh and Henry Hamilton, Drury Lane, 1909. Typical of the Autumn Dramas which had become established at the Lane from the 1880s, all full of spectacular scenic effects and stirring melodramatic plots. (Photograph: Foulsham and Banfield)

128 LEFT *Monsieur Beaucaire*. Lewis Waller and Grace Lane in the romantic comedy by Booth Tarkington, Comedy Theatre, 1902. Waller became the first matinee idol to have a 'fan' club, 'The Keen on Waller's' (The K.O.W.'s). He produced a series of romantic costume dramas which achieved great popularity. (Photograph: The London Stereoscopic Company)

129 *The Sins of Society* by Cecil Raleigh and Henry
Hamilton, Drury Lane, 1907. A lavish *art nouveau* set by
Henry Emden in an Autumn Drama which was revived in
1911. (Photograph: The *Daily Mirror* Studios)

130 The Ellen Terry Jubilee Performance, Drury Lane,
12 June 1906. Ellen Terry, with her sisters Marian and
Kate, surrounded by members of their family in the Mask
Scene from *Much Ado About Nothing*. The setting and
costumes are those from the 1903 production by Gordon
Craig at the Imperial Theatre. (Photograph: The Dover
Street Studios)

131 The Ellen Terry Jubilee Performance, Drury Lane, 1906. The Picture Gallery Scene from *The School for Scandal*. Every famous player and actor-manager paid tribute to Ellen Terry at this performance. In this group Bourchier, Wyndham, Alexander and Weedon Grossmith may be identified. (Photograph: The Dover Street Studios)

132 LEFT *Our Miss Gibbs*, a musical comedy at The Gaiety Theatre, 1909. The Gaiety Girls sing the chorus of 'Yip-I-Addy-I-Ay' in a scene at the White City Exhibition. (Photograph: Foulsham and Banfield)

PARADISE, IN THE VALHALLA OF STAGE CELEBRITIES.

133 LEFT *The Merry Widow*, Daly's Theatre, 1907. Lehar's Viennese operetta turned into an English musical comedy: the scene at Maxims, with George Graves and Lily Elsie as Popoff and Sonia. (Photograph: Foulsham and Banfield)

134 ABOVE Paradise in the Valhalla of Stage Celebrities. A Raphael Tuck postcard montage, 1910. The actresses from left to right are: Marie Wilson, Cressie Leonard, Alice Russon, Nina Sevening, Sybil Arundale, Evie Greene, Miriam Clements, Jean Aylwin, Thelma Raye, Olive May, Kitty Gordon, Kitty Mason, Jessie Rose and Florence Ward. Picture postcards of theatrical celebrities began to appear at the turn of the century and by 1910 had become a thriving industry

135 ABOVE *Jack and the Beanstalk*, Shakespeare Theatre, Liverpool, 1908. The Grand Finale with Ada Reeve as Jack. Pantomime retained a firm hold on the provinces, and productions remained traditional outside London for many years

136 LEFT *Venus 1906*, a revue at the Empire Theatre, London. Early in the century attempts were made to introduce French *Revue* to the music hall stage, but it did not become firmly established until the advent of Ragtime in 1912. (Photograph: Ellis and Walery)

137 ABOVE Phyllis Dare as Cinderella, Newcastle, 1906. One of the great picture postcard beauties of the day – who, with her sister Zena, vied for popular acclaim with Gabrielle Ray, Marie Studholme and Mabel Love

138 ABOVE 'A morning rehearsal', 1900

139 BELOW Julia Nielson leaving the theatre after a rehearsal, Comedy Theatre, 1904

140 ABOVE The leading lady's dressing-room, Daly's
Theatre, 1901 : Florence Collingbourne preparing to play
San Toy

141 BELOW The audience leaving after a matinee of *The
Wilderness*, St James's Theatre, 1901

142 ABOVE *L'Amour*, a ballet at the Alhambra Theatre, 1906, with Marie Bordini. (Photograph: Campbell Gray)

143 LEFT Adeline Genée in *The Dryad*, Empire Theatre, 1908

144 Isadora Duncan introduces Greek barefoot dancing, 1908

145 Enrico Caruso as Don José in *Carmen*. The greatest tenor of his generation, Caruso made his Covent Garden début in 1902. His voice was made immortal by the gramophone. (Photograph: Aimé Dupont)

ADELINA PATTI · MADAME MELBA · Mme TETRAZZINI · MADAME ALBANI

SIGNOR CARUSO · EDWARD LLOYD · M^r BEN DAVIES

Mrs KENNERLEY RUMFORD · EDNA THORNTON · MISS ADA CROSSLEY · MADAME KIRKBY LUNN

Mr ANDREW BLACK · S^{ir} CHARLES SANTLEY · Mr WATKIN MILLS

Mr ROBERT RADFORD · Mr KENNERLEY RUMFORD · Mr JOHN COATES · J C McCORMACK

7121 I   SOME FAMOUS VOCALISTS ·   ROTARY PHOTO. E C

146 'Some Famous Vocalists': a picture postcard souvenir,
1908

VESTA TILLEY

MARIE, LLOYD

NETTIE KING

GEORGE ROBEY

LITTLE TICH

HARRY LAUDER

MARGARET COOPER

WILKIE BARD

MAUD ALLAN

7121 **G**   SOME FAMOUS MUSIC HALL STARS.   ROTARY PHOTO F.C

147 'Some famous Music Hall Stars': a picture postcard
souvenir, 1908

148 ABOVE The Granville, Walham Green, 1902. A Frank Matcham music hall, opened in 1898

149 BELOW Waiting for the first house at the London Pavilion, 1902

150 ABOVE The Gallery at the Metropolitan Music Hall,
Edgware Road, 1902

151 BELOW 'In the Wings: waiting to go on', Royal Music
Hall, Holborn, 1902

152 ABOVE 'All the Fun of the Fair.' St Giles Fair, Oxford, 1908

GARRETT'S
EMPIRE ~~DULY LICENCED PURSUANT TO~~ THEATRE
~~ACT OF PARLIAMENT TO PERFORM~~
~~STAGE PLAYS IN THEIR ENTIRETY~~

154 Garrett's Empire Theatre, 1908. The company outside a
wooden portable theatre which had toured the country
since the 1890s, playing stock melodramas and Shakespeare
with a nightly change of bill. They were considered 'a cut
above' the fairground portables

153 LEFT Studt's Portable Theatre at a fair, 1908. By the
turn of the century, many showmen were turning towards
Moving Pictures in what had originally been booth
theatres, but continuing the traditional live methods of
attracting an audience

155 'Hi! Hi! Now for the Coconuts! Roll or bowl a ball, a Penny a Pitch', 1908

156 RIGHT Consulting the Oracle: 'Is Marriage a Failure – Try the Fairy Press', 1908, with picture postcards as bait

157 Stratford-upon-Avon Mop Fair, 1908; held annually
for centuries in the streets of the town on 12 October and
only recently banished from the town centre. These
roundabouts and sideshows are grouped around the
American Memorial Fountain in the Market Place

158 Stratford-upon-Avon Sports Day, 1908: 'Mowing the Barley'. Outside the first Shakespeare Memorial Theatre, by the Gower Memorial

159 Hampstead Heath, Bank Holiday, 1904: 'knees-up'
outside The Old Bull and Bush

160 LEFT The Oxford Pageant, 1907: the arrival of Queen
Henrietta Maria. 'O, call back yesterday, bid Time return.'
Shakespeare quoted in the souvenir programme.
Centennials and historic occasions were celebrated by local
amateurs up and down the country at the slightest
provocation throughout the Edwardian period

161 ABOVE York Historical Pageant, 1909: the final tableau.
'A good time was had by all', *vide* Local Press

162 Pierrots on the sands at Clacton, 1908

163 Billy Keen's 'famous' Pierrot Party, Portrush, 1906

164 The 'Smart Set' entertains, 1909. While the Pierrots were mainly on the sands, the more sophisticated entertainers occupied the pier pavilions

165 The Pier, Hastings, 1905. The famous Mohawk Minstrels, banished from London, ended their career at the end of the pier

166 Nigger Minstrels on the sands at Scarborough, 1900

167 Nigger Minstrels in the street, Eastbourne, 1909. From
a late stereoscopic slide

168 ABOVE LEFT Paris in London at Earl's Court, 1902. Spectacular exhibitions, often directed by the Kinalfy Brothers, were a feature of later Victorian and Edwardian London. The Big Wheel at Earl's Court was one of the Wonders of 1896, and remained a feature for many years

169 LEFT The Franco–British Exhibition of 1908 at The White City, Shepherd's Bush. Yet another example of the *entente cordiale* exhibitions of Edwardian days

170 ABOVE The Water Chute, Crystal Palace, 1902

171 The Motor Show, 1907, at Olympia, which was built in 1884 as an exhibition centre; every conceivable kind of entertainment was presented within its walls: circus, Royal Tournaments, horse shows, pageants and spectacles

172 'The Scorcher Held Up', 1903. Evie Greene and friend, caught on a picture postcard at the beginning of the new motoring craze

E., "THE SCORCHER HELD UP"   ROTARY PHOTO. E.C.   199.G

Photographers Represented

173 'Wait and See'. A picture postcard of 1910. An early strip-tease, and prelude to a new era of entertainment